3-MINUTE
DEVOTIONS
FOR WOMEN

Large Print Edition

D1500157

ISBN 978-1-68322-609-3

Readings are compiled from books from the 3-Minute Devotions for Women series, including *Choose Grace*, *Choose Hope*, *Choose Joy*, and *Choose Prayer*.

Published by Barbour Books, an imprint of Barbour Publishing, Inc., 1810 Barbour Drive, Uhrichsville, Ohio 44683, www.barbourbooks.com

Our mission is to inspire the world with the life-changing message of the Bible.

Member of the
Evangelical Christian
Publishers Association

3-MINUTE DEVOTIONS

DEVOTIONS

FOR WOMEN

Large Print Edition

BARBOUR BOOKS

An Imprint of Barbour Publishing, Inc.

INTRODUCTION

Most days we're seeking out a moment or two of inspiration and encouragement—a fresh breath of air for the lungs and soul.

Here is a collection of moments from the true Source of all inspiration and encouragement—God's Word. Within these pages, you'll be guided through just-right-sized readings that you can experience in three minutes:

Minute 1: Reflect on God's Word

Minute 2: Read real-life application and encouragement

Minute 3: Pray

These devotions aren't meant to be a replacement for digging deep into the scriptures or for personal quiet time. Instead, consider them a perfect jump-start to help you form a habit of spending time with God every day. Or add them to the time you're already spending with Him. Share these moments with friends, family, coworkers, and others you come in contact with every day. They're looking for inspiration and encouragement too.

∙∙∙

Your word is a lamp to guide my feet and a light for my path.
PSALM 119:105 NLT

Even More!

Now unto him that is able to do exceeding abundantly above all that we ask or think, according to the power that worketh in us. . .

Ephesians 3:20 KJV

"Above all that we ask or think" is just that. Imagine every good thing that God has promised in His Word—or things you've only dreamed about. Think of wonderful things that exceed the limits of human comprehension or description then imagine that God is able and willing to do even more!

The last part of this verse indicates that the Holy Spirit works within the Christian's life to accomplish the seemingly impossible. Our highest aspirations are within God's power—but like Paul, we must pray. When we do, God does far more for us than we could ever guess.

Oh Lord, You accomplish things
I perceive as impossible. You
know my hopes and dreams, and I
believe that You are able to exceed
my greatest expectations. Amen.

He Will Send Help

....

*"The waves of death swirled about
me; the torrents of destruction
overwhelmed me. . . . In my distress
I called to the L*ord*. . . . From his
temple he heard my voice;
my cry came to his ears."*
2 Samuel 22:5, 7 NIV

....

God never asked us to do life alone.
When the waves of death swirl
around us, and the pounding rain of
destruction threatens to overwhelm
us, we can cry out to our heavenly
Father, knowing that He will not let us

drown. He will hear our voice, and He will send help. So, next time you feel that you can't put one foot in front of the other, ask God to send you His strength and energy. He will help you to live out your purpose in this chaotic world.

*Lord, thank You for strengthening
me when the dailiness of life,
and its various trials, threatens
to overwhelm me. Amen.*

STEADY. . .

People with their minds set on you, you keep completely whole, steady on their feet, because they keep at it and don't quit.
ISAIAH 26:3 MSG

One of the meanings of *grace* is "an effortless beauty of movement." A person with this kind of grace doesn't trip over her own feet; she's not clumsy or awkward, but instead she moves easily, fluidly, steadily. From a spiritual perspective, most of us stumble quite a bit—and yet we don't give up. We know that God holds our hands, and He will keep us steady even when we would otherwise fall flat on our faces.

Father, I don't always feel so graceful. Thank You for holding my hand, steadying my feet, and giving me the strength to keep at it, even when I stumble. Amen.

Every Step of the Way

Never stop praying.
1 Thessalonians 5:17 NLT

Several passages in the Bible tell us clearly that God listens to us when we pray. He hears every word and is compassionate. All we have to do is share our concerns with Him and wait faithfully for what He will provide.

God wants to be involved in our daily routines. He wants to hear from us and waits for us. God never promised an easy life to Christians. If we will allow Him, though, God will be there with us every step of the way. All we need to do is to come to Him in prayer. With these three simple words from 1 Thessalonians 5:17, our lives can be fulfilling as we live to communicate with our Lord.

Father, when I pray remind me that prayer is not only about talking to You, but also about listening to You. Open my heart to Your words. Amen.

Reveal the Hope

In your hearts revere Christ as Lord. Always be prepared to give an answer to everyone who asks you to give the reason for the hope that you have. But do this with gentleness and respect.
1 Peter 3:15 NIV

Isn't the relevance of God's Word amazing? Peter gives three parts of advice with several key words. First, Peter advises, set God apart from everything else in your heart; in other words, "sanctify," or recognize God's holiness, and treat Him with deserved awe. Second, be prepared to explain your hope in Christ and eternal life, having a full grasp of what, and in whom, you believe. Finally, remember *how* you say something is equally important to *what* you say. In other words, we must walk the walk before we can reveal the hope we have in Jesus Christ.

Dear God, please prepare me to explain my hope in Christ and eternal life. Teach me to explain it in a way that honors You with gentleness and respect. Amen.

SHAKE IT UP!

*The L*ORD *had said to Abram,*
"Leave your native country, your
relatives, and your father's family,
and go to the land that I will show
you. . . . I will bless you. . .and
you will be a blessing to others."
GENESIS 12:1–2 NLT

In God's wisdom, He likes to shake us up a little, stretch us out of our comfort zone, push us out on a limb. Yet we resist the change, cling to what's known, and try to change His mind with fat, sloppy tears. Are you facing a big change? God wants us to be willing to embrace change that He brings into our lives. Even unbidden change. You may feel as if you're out on a limb, but don't forget that God is the tree trunk. He's not going to let you fall.

Holy, loving Father, in every area of my life, teach me to trust You more deeply. Amen.

FREE!

For the Lord is the Spirit,
and wherever the Spirit of
the Lord is, there is freedom.
2 CORINTHIANS 3:17 NLT

How do you know when the Holy Spirit is present in your life? You should be able to tell by the sense of freedom you feel. If you feel oppressed, obsessed, or depressed, something in your life is off-kilter. Seek out God's Spirit. He wants you to be free.

Holy Spirit, fill me with a sense of freedom only You can provide. Free my spirit from chains of oppression, and draw me into the wide open spaces of Your peace. Amen.

STILLNESS

....

Be still, and know that I am God.
PSALM 46:10 NKJV

....

David wrote, "Meditate within your heart on your bed, and be still" (Psalm 4:4 NKJV). Many of us have lost the ability to meditate on God. We either tell ourselves that meditation is something only Buddhist monks do, or else we cry out frantic prayers while distracted by the careening roller coaster of life. When we lie down in bed at night, instead of meditating calmly and trusting in God, we fret and toss and turn.

When we learn to trust that God can protect us and work out our problems, then we can lie down peacefully and sleep (Psalm 4:8). That same trust gives us the strength to face our days with confidence.

Dear God, quiet my mind. Remove from it all the worldly thoughts that come between You and me. Create stillness within me, and turn my thoughts toward You. Amen.

PLANTED DEEP

Fix these words of mine in your hearts and minds; tie them as symbols on your hands and bind them on your foreheads.

DEUTERONOMY 11:18 NIV

Memorizing Bible verses isn't a fashionable trend in today's world, but learning key verses plants the Word of God deeply in our hearts. We draw strength and nourishment in dark times from remembering what God told us in the Bible. In times of crisis we recall God's promises of hope and comfort. In our everyday moments, repeating well-known verses reminds us that God is always with us—whether we feel like it or not.

What an awesome gift You have given me, God—the Bible! I will fix Your words in my mind and heart and carry them with me wherever I go. Amen.

Release the
Music Within

∙∙

*Those who are wise will find a time
and a way to do what is right.*
Ecclesiastes 8:5 nlt

∙∙

It has been said that many people go to their graves with their music still in them. Do you carry a song within your heart, waiting to be heard?

Whether we are eight or eighty, it is never too late to surrender our hopes and dreams to God. A wise woman trusts that God will help her find the time and manner in which to use her talents for His glory as she seeks His direction. Let the music begin.

Dear Lord, my music is fading against the constant beat of a busy pace. I surrender my gifts to You and pray for the time and manner in which I can use those gifts to touch my world. Amen.

LOOK UP!

....

Your love, LORD,
reaches to the heavens,
your faithfulness to the skies.
PSALM 36:5 NIV

....

In Bible times, people often studied the sky. Looking up at the heavens reminded them of God and His mighty wonders. A rainbow was God's sign to Noah that a flood would never again destroy the earth. God used a myriad of stars to foretell Abraham's abundant family, and a single star heralded Christ's birth. This immense space that we call "sky" is a reflection of God's infinite love and faithfulness. So take time today. Look up at the heavens, and thank God for His endless love.

Heavenly Father, remind me to stop and appreciate Your wonderful creations. And as I look upward, fill me with Your infinite love. Amen.

THY WILL BE DONE

···

He went away a second time and prayed, "My Father, if it is not possible for this cup to be taken away unless I drink it, may your will be done."
MATTHEW 26:42 NIV

···

Jesus didn't ask this just once—He made this request three times in Matthew 26. These red-letter prayers reveal the 100 percent human side of Jesus.

In one of His darkest hours, Jesus was overwhelmed with sorrow. He asked God for something that God would not provide. But Jesus, perfect and obedient, ended His prayers by saying, "*Your* will be done."

When we face our darkest hours, will we follow Jesus' example? Can we submit to God's perfect will, focusing on how much He loves us—even when His will doesn't match ours?

I wonder why You refuse when I ask for what I think is right. But Your knowledge is greater than my understanding. So, Thy will be done, God. Thy perfect will be done. Amen.

KNOW THE HOPE

I pray that the eyes of your heart may be enlightened in order that you may know the hope to which he has called you, the riches of his glorious inheritance in his holy people, and his incomparably great power for us who believe.
EPHESIANS 1:18–19 NIV

Our heart is central when it comes to God. It's not only vital for our physical life but our spiritual life as well. It's the thinking apparatus of our soul, containing all our thoughts, passions, and desires. Why was Paul so anxious for Christians to make heartfelt spiritual progress? Because of the payoff! God freely offers us his incomparably great power along with a rich, glorious inheritance. We just have to see our need for a little surgery.

Instill in me a new heart, God. Fill it with Your unrivaled power and love. Place within it the priceless gift of Jesus' sacrifice and the promise of eternal life in heaven. Amen.

SIMPLY SILLY

*A cheerful disposition
is good for your health.*
PROVERBS 17:22 MSG

Imagine the effect we could have on our world today if our countenance reflected the joy of the Lord all the time: at work, at home, at play. Jesus said, "I have told you this so that my joy may be in you and that your joy may be complete" (John 15:11 NIV). Is your cup of joy full? Have you laughed today? Not a small smile, but laughter. Maybe it's time we looked for something to laugh about and tasted joy. Jesus suggested it.

Lord, help me find joy this day. Let me laugh and give praises to the King. Amen.

Amazing Expectations

*Listen to my voice in the
morning, Lord. Each morning
I bring my requests to you
and wait expectantly.*
PSALM 5:3 NLT

You need to get in the habit of hoping. Instead of getting up in the morning and sighing as you face another dreary day, practice saying hello to God as soon as you wake up. Listen for what He wants to say to your heart. Expect Him to do amazing things each day.

Good morning, Lord. I can easily forget how necessary it is to begin my day in sweet communion with You. Tune my heart's ear to the lovely sound of Your voice. Amen.

GOD ALREADY KNOWS

*"As soon as you began
to pray, a word went out,
which I have come to tell you,
for you are highly esteemed."*
DANIEL 9:23 NIV

While pouring out his heart to God one day, Daniel's prayer is interrupted by the angel Gabriel. Bringing insight and understanding (v. 22), Gabriel's message contains the interesting concept that in the instant that Daniel began to pray, the answer was already on its way.

Before Daniel got past his

salutation, God knew Daniel's heart and had already set in motion the response to Daniel's unfinished prayer.

As He did for Daniel, God knows our needs even before we give voice to them in prayer. We can rest in the knowledge that even before the words leave our lips, God has already heard them, and He has already answered them.

Thank You, God, for answering my prayers. Before the words leave my lips, You already have the answer. How great You are, God! I praise You. Amen.

GOD HEARS

I love the LORD because he hears my voice and my prayer for mercy.
PSALM 116:1 NLT

Psalm 116:1 is a wonderful verse that should not be missed. It is neither lament nor praise, as are many of the other psalms. But it is a strong assurance of hope. Whether we are offering our praise to God or falling at His feet with our struggles, we know from these few words that God hears us. Isn't that mind-blowing? The almighty God of the universe who created and assembled every particle in existence hears us when we come before Him.

I have so many reasons to love You, Lord, so many reasons to worship and praise You. How grateful I am that You hear my voice! I love You, Lord. Amen.

ANXIOUS ANTICIPATIONS

*I am not saying this because
I am in need, for I have
learned to be content
whatever the circumstances.*

PHILIPPIANS 4:11 NIV

Have you ever been so eager for the future that you forgot to be thankful for the present day?

Humans have a tendency to complain about the problems and irritations of life. It's much less natural to appreciate the good things we have—until they're gone. While it's fine to look forward to the future, let's remember to reflect on all of *today's* blessings—the large and the small—and appreciate all that we do have.

Thank You, Lord, for the beauty of today. Please remind me when I become preoccupied with the future and forget to enjoy the present. Amen.

Open Homes

*Be quick to give a meal
to the hungry, a bed to
the homeless—cheerfully.*
1 Peter 4:9 MSG

Because our homes are our private places, the places we retreat to when we're too tired to find new strength, it's hard sometimes to open our homes to others. It's bad enough that we have to cope with others' needs all day long, we feel, without having to bring them home with us! But God calls us to offer our hospitality, and He will give us the grace to do it joyfully.

God, You have blessed me with a home—a sanctuary. And I am so grateful for it. Help me to joyfully share that blessing with others. Amen.

Be Anxious for Nothing

• •

*Be anxious for nothing,
but in everything by prayer
and supplication, with
thanksgiving, let your requests
be made known to God.*
Philippians 4:6 NKJV

• •

"Be anxious for nothing" sounds like great advice, but at times most of us have the feeling that it only works for highly mature saints and is not practical for the average Christian.

Yet the key to making it work is

found in the same verse. We can "be anxious for nothing" if we are continually taking those problems to God in prayer, thanking Him for solving past problems, and trusting Him to work the current situation out. Praying about things, of course, shouldn't keep us from doing what God inspires us to do to solve the problems. But we should trust and pray instead of fretting and worrying.

Father, anxiety makes me weary. Today I ask You to take all my problems and work them out for good. Amen.

Renewed Hope and Faith

....

I am Alpha and Omega,
the beginning and the end,
the first and the last.
Revelation 22:13 KJV

....

In the Old Testament, the Lord God called Himself a Shepherd, the Alpha and Omega, the Beginning and the End, and the Almighty. He is called the First and the Last. In the New Testament, we find the same titles given to Jesus. The Bible is unique because in it God fully reveals who

He is. Since Jesus is fully God, let it renew our hope and faith in our Savior. He who created all things out of nothing will re-create this world into a paradise without sin.

Jesus, I learn how to live by Your human example, and I trust in You as my God—Father, Son, and Holy Spirit—three persons, one God, one perfect You! Amen.

Refreshing Gift

....

*For we have great joy and
consolation in your love, because
the hearts of the saints have been
refreshed by you, brother.*
Philemon 1:7 NKJV

....

Jesus always took the time for those
who reached out to Him. In a crowd of
people, He stopped to help a woman
who touched Him. His quiet love
extended to everyone who asked,
whether verbally or with unspoken
need. God brings people into our path
who need our encouragement. We

must consider those around us. Smile and thank the waiter, the cashier, the people who help in small ways. Cheering others can have the effect of an energizing drink of water so that they will be able to finish the race with a smile.

Jesus, thank You for being an example of how to encourage and refresh others. Help me to see their need and to be willing to reach out. Amen.

LETTING GO

A peaceful heart leads to a healthy body; jealousy is like cancer in the bones.

PROVERBS 14:30 NLT

Some emotions are meant to be nourished, and others need to be quickly dropped into God's hands. Learn to cultivate and seek out that which brings peace to your heart. And practice letting go of your negative feelings as quickly as you can, releasing them to God. If you cling to these dark feelings, they will reproduce like a cancer, blocking the healthy flow of grace into your life.

Oh God, search me and know my heart. Expose any negative feelings in me. Help me to leave them at the cross. Cleanse me and fill my heart with Your peace. Amen.

When Words Fail Me

• •

Before a word is on my tongue you,
Lord, know it completely.
Psalm 139:4 NIV

• •

Sometimes Christians feel so overwhelmed by their needs or by the greatness of God that they simply can't pray. When the words won't come, God helps to create them. Paul says in Romans 8:26 (NLT), "And the Holy Spirit helps us in our weakness. For example, we don't know what God wants us to pray for. But the Holy Spirit prays for us with groanings that cannot be expressed in words."

God hears your prayers even before you pray them. When you don't know what to say and the words won't come, you can simply ask God to help you by praying on your behalf.

Dear God, I'm grateful today
that in my silence You
still hear me. Amen.

HOPE THRIVES

"For I know the plans I have for you,"
declares the LORD, "plans to prosper
you and not to harm you, plans to
give you hope and a future."

JEREMIAH 29:11 NIV

Hope thrives in the fertile soil of a heart restored by a loving gesture, a compassionate embrace, or an encouraging word. It is one of God's most precious gifts. God *wants* to forgive our sins and lead us on the paths of righteousness—just as He did for the Israelites of old. He has great plans for us. That's His promise, and our blessed hope.

Father, You provide hope when all seems hopeless. Trusting in Your plans for me brings me joy. My future is in Your hands, so how can it be anything but good? Amen.

INFINITE AND PERSONAL

Am I a God at hand, saith the
LORD, and not a God afar off? . . .
Do not I fill heaven and earth?
JEREMIAH 23:23–24 KJV

God says that He is both close at hand and over all there is. Whether your day is crumbling around you or is the best day you have ever had, do you see God in it? If the "sky is falling" or the sun is shining, do you still recognize the One who orders all the planets and all your days? Whether we see Him or not, God tells

us He is there. And He's here too—
in the good times and bad.

*Lord, empower me to trust You when
it's hard to remember that You are
near. And help me to live thankfully
when times are good. Amen.*

Open to Joy

"The joy of the Lord
is your strength."
Nehemiah 8:10 niv

Our God is a God of joy. He is not a God of sighing and gloom. Open yourself to His joy. It is a gift of grace He longs to give you. He knows it will make you strong.

Oh Lord, giver of joy and source of my strength, thank You for these gifts, which are mine in abundance. Help me to rely on Your joy and strength. Amen.

CALL ON ME

"Call on me in the day of trouble;
I will deliver you,
and you will honor me."
PSALM 50:15 NIV

When God says He wants us to call Him, He means it. He must lean closer, bending His ear, waiting, longing for the sound of His name coming from our lips. He stands ready to deliver us from our troubles or at least to carry us through them safely.

While He doesn't always choose to fix things with a snap of His fingers, we can be assured that He will see us through to the other side of our troubles by a smoother path than we'd travel without Him. He's waiting to help us. All we have to do is call.

Dear Father, I'm so glad I can call on You anytime with any kind of trouble. Amen.

LOVE SONG OF FORGIVENESS

·······································

*"In that day," declares the LORD,
"you will call me 'my husband'; you
will no longer call me 'my master.'"*

HOSEA 2:16 NIV

·······································

God wants *our* hearts. He desires a relationship with us based on love and forgiveness. He enters into a covenant with us, like the marriage between Hosea and Gomer. God is the loving, faithful husband, constantly pursuing us no matter what we do or where we roam. Though it is difficult to grasp how much He loves us, we find hope in His promise. God will keep his commitment to us. His love song to us is forgiveness, and His wedding vow is unconditional love.

Thank You for loving me so fully and unconditionally, God. I find comfort knowing that as much as any man on Earth could love me, You love me more. Amen.

WALK CONFIDENTLY

....

"But blessed are those who trust in the LORD and have made the LORD their hope and confidence."
JEREMIAH 17:7 NLT

....

What gives you confidence? Is it your clothes. . .your money. . .your skills? These are all good things, but they are blessings from God, given to you through His grace. When your hopes (in other words, your expectations for the future) rest only in God, then you can walk confidently, knowing He will never disappoint you.

Lord, You are my hope and my confidence. I place all my expectations for the future in You, knowing that You will never disappoint me. Thank You for Your love. Amen.

GROUNDED IN LOVE

*"You'll be built solid, grounded
in righteousness, far from any
trouble—nothing to fear!"*
ISAIAH 54:12 MSG

Balance isn't something we can achieve in ourselves. Just when we think we have it all together, life has a tendency to come crashing down around our ears. But even in the midst of life's most chaotic moments, God gives us grace; He keeps us balanced in His love. Like a building that is built to sway in an earthquake without falling down, we will stay standing if we remain grounded in His love.

Heavenly Father, keep me grounded in Your love. Provide for me a strong foundation to keep me stable through life's most chaotic moments. Thank You for Your steady hand. Amen.

PRAY INSTEAD OF PLOTTING

*"Pray that the Lord your
God will show us what
to do and where to go."*
JEREMIAH 42:3 NLT

However bleak your situation seems, God hasn't forgotten you. Philippians 4:6–7 (NLT) says, "Don't worry about anything; instead, pray about everything. Tell God what you need, and thank him for all he has done. Then you will experience God's peace, which exceeds anything we can understand. His peace will guard your hearts and minds as you live in Christ Jesus."

Jeremiah 42:3 echoes this statement. It urges believers to pray for guidance instead of setting out with a preconceived notion of how the day (or month or decade) will turn out.

When you begin to worry that you don't have what it takes to meet life's demands, remember that you don't have to—because God does.

Jesus, thank You for Your presence and the peace You so freely give. Help me to pray before I worry, categorize, or strategize. Amen.

ONLY BELIEVE

....

While Jesus was still speaking,
some people came from the house
of Jairus, the synagogue leader.
"Your daughter is dead," they said.
"Why bother the teacher anymore?"
MARK 5:35 NIV

....

When the odds are stacked against us and circumstances riddle us with hopelessness, our tendency is to manage our burdens as well as we can and stop praying. Doubtful, we wonder: Can God restore an unhappy marriage? Can He heal cancer? Can

He deliver me from financial ruin? *Will* He? Jesus knows the way out. Only believe; have faith in Him and never lose hope.

Jesus, my hope is in You. Even when it appears that all hope is lost, I will hold onto the hope that You will deliver me. Amen.

GOD IN THE DETAILS

∙∙∙

"When we heard of it, our hearts melted in fear and everyone's courage failed because of you, for the LORD your God is God in heaven above and on the earth below."

JOSHUA 2:11 NIV

∙∙∙

Sometimes, when our lives seem to be under siege from the demands of work, bills, family, whatever— finding the work of God amid the strife can be difficult. Even though we acknowledge His power, we may

72

overlook the gentle touches, the small ways in which He makes every day a little easier. Just as the Lord cares for the tiniest bird (Matthew 10:29–31), so He seeks to be a part of every detail in your life. Look for Him there.

Father God, I know You are by my side every day, good or bad, and that You love and care for me. Help me to see Your work in my life and in the lives of my friends and family. Amen.

Transformed

....

And Sarah declared, "God has brought me laughter. All who hear about this will laugh with me."
GENESIS 21:6 NLT

....

The first time we read of Sarah laughing, it was because she doubted God. She didn't believe that at her age she would have a baby. But God didn't hold her laughter against her. Instead, He transformed it. He turned her laughter of scorn and doubt into the laughter of fulfillment and grace.

*Father Redeemer, thank You
for taking my very worst moments
and transforming them into a story
You can use for Your purpose
and Your glory. Amen.*

ARROW PRAYERS

....

God knows how often I pray for you. Day and night I bring you and your needs in prayer to God.
ROMANS 1:9 NLT

....

Our prayers are often lost in the obscurity of brevity. We love fast food and instant success. All the while we struggle to take the time to utter a few extra syllables to God. We shoot "arrow" prayers while expecting God's response ASAP. We expect the Lord, who knows all, to interpret our every need.

Although arrow prayers are sometimes needed, God asks us to pray *specifically* and often for the person or problem just as Paul did. God made us to fellowship with Him. That includes open communication void of brevity mania!

Lord, forgive me for my abbreviated prayers, void of substance and heart. Teach me to pray in specifics and less in generalities as I openly pour out my innermost needs and desires to You. Amen.

SEEKING GOD'S PLAN

*For we are His workmanship,
created in Christ Jesus for
good works, which God
prepared beforehand that
we should walk in them.*

EPHESIANS 2:10 NKJV

How can you know God's plans for your life? First, you should meet with Him in prayer each day and seek His will. Studying the Bible is also important. Often, God speaks to us directly through His Word (Psalm 119:105). Finally, you must have faith that God *will* work out His plan for your life and that His plan is good. Jeremiah 29:11 (NIV) says, "'For I know the plans I have for you,' declares the LORD, 'plans to prosper you and not to harm you, plans to give you hope and a future.'" Are you living in Christ's example and seeking God's plan for your life?

Father, what is Your plan for me? I know that it is good. Reveal it to me, Lord. Speak to me through prayer and Your Word. Amen.

PRACTICALITY VS. PASSION

....

*Leaving her water jar, the woman
went back to the town and said to
the people, "Come, see a man
who told me everything I ever did.
Could this be the Messiah?"*
JOHN 4:28–29 NIV

....

Practicality gave way to passion the
day the woman at the well abandoned
her task, laid down her jar, and ran into
town. Everything changed the day she
met a man at the well and He asked
her for a drink of water. Although they

had never met before, He told her everything she had ever done, and then He offered her living water that would never run dry. Do you live with such passion, or do you cling to your water jar? Has an encounter with Christ made an impact that cannot be denied in your life?

Lord, help me to lay down anything that stifles my passion for sharing the Good News with others. Amen.

10 Percent

The earth is the Lord's,
and everything in it.
Psalm 24:1 NLT

Do you tithe? Giving 10 percent of your income specifically to God's work is a good discipline. But sometimes we act as though that 10 percent is God's and the other 90 percent is ours. We forget that everything is God's. Through grace, He shares all of creation with us. When we look at it that way, our 10 percent tithe seems a little stingy!

Heavenly Father, everything belongs to You—even the cattle on a thousand hills. Thank You for sharing Your wealth with me, and help me to share it lavishly with others. Amen.

Solitary Prayer

*Come near to God and
he will come near to you.*
JAMES 4:8 NIV

Do you have a prayer closet?

Jesus warned against people praying in public with the intent to show others how pious they are. Instead, He advocated solitude. Jesus often went off by Himself to draw near to His Father and pray, and that is what He suggested in the passage from Matthew.

A secret room isn't necessary—rather a quiet place where one can be alone with God. Maybe your quiet place is your garden or the beach. It might be in the quiet of your own home when your husband and children are away. Wherever it is, enjoy some time alone with God. Draw near to Him in prayer, and He will draw near to you.

Dear God, when we meet in the quiet place, allow me to breathe in Your presence. Amen.

BEHIND THE SCENES

···

*Now faith is the substance of
things hoped for, the evidence
of things not seen.*
HEBREWS 11:1 NKJV

···

Be encouraged today that no matter
what takes place in the natural—what
you see with your eyes—it doesn't
have to be the final outcome of your
situation. If you've asked God for
something, then you can trust that
He is working out all the details
behind the scenes.

What you see right now, how you

feel, is not a picture of what your faith is producing. Your faith is active, and God is busy working to make all things come together and benefit you.

Heavenly Father, what I see today is not what I'm going to get. Thank You for working behind the scenes to bring about the very best for my life. Amen.

Lord, you are my God; I will exalt you and praise your name, for in perfect faithfulness you have done wonderful things, things planned long ago.
Isaiah 25:1 NIV

God has a "promised land" for us all—a marvelous plan for our lives. Recount and record His faithfulness in your life in the past, because God has already demonstrated His marvelous plans to you in so many ways. Then prayerfully anticipate the future journey with Him. Keep a record of

God's marvelous plans in a journal as He unfolds them day by day. You will find God to be faithful in the smallest aspects of your life and oh so worthy of your trust.

Oh Lord, help me to recount Your faithfulness, record Your faithfulness, and trust Your faithfulness in the future.
For You are my God, and You have done marvelous things, things planned long ago. Amen.

LOVING SUPPORT

······································

Let us think of ways to motivate one another to acts of love and good works.
HEBREWS 10:24 NLT

······································

Imagine that you're sitting in the bleachers watching one of your favorite young people play a sport. You jump up and cheer for him. You make sure he knows you're there, shouting out encouragement. Hearing your voice, he jumps higher, runs faster. That is the sort of excitement and support we need to show others around us.

When we do all we can to encourage each other, love and good deeds will burst from us all.

Lord, help me to be a cheerleader for others. Help me to see the world through their eyes and to say and do the things I know would motivate and encourage them. Amen.

STAYING ON TRACK

I have fought a good fight,
I have finished my course,
I have kept the faith.
2 TIMOTHY 4:7 KJV

Despite the pain and afflictions Paul suffered in his life, he kept his eyes on Jesus, using praise to commune with God.

Likewise, we can keep in constant communion with the Father. We are so blessed to have been given the Holy Spirit within to keep us in tune with His will. Through His guidance, that still, small voice, we can rest assured our priorities will stay focused on Jesus. As the author A. W. Tozer wrote, "Lord, guide me carefully on this uncharted sea. . .as I daily seek You in Your word. Then use me mightily as Your servant this year as I boldly proclaim Your word in leading others."

Lord, no better words have
been spoken than to say
I surrender to Your will. Amen.

RELEASING YOUR HOLD ON ANXIETY

....

Search me, O God, and know my heart; test me and know my anxious thoughts. See if there is any offensive way in me, and lead me in the way everlasting.
PSALM 139:23–24 NIV

....

What is it that weighs you down? Financial issues? An unhealthy relationship? Your busy schedule? Surrender these misgivings to a God who wants to take them from you. Ask Him to search your heart for any and all anxieties, for any and all signs that you have not truly put your trust in Him. Find the trouble spots in your life to which you direct most of your thoughts and energy, and then hand these troubles over to the One who can truly address them.

Realize that you are only human, and that God is infinitely more capable of balancing your cares than you are.

Lord, take from me my anxieties, big and small. May I remember to give these to You daily so that I will not find myself distracted by the things of this world. Amen.

LIFE PRESERVERS

My comfort in my suffering is this:
Your promise preserves my life.
PSALM 119:50 NIV

In the difficulties of life, God is our life preserver. When we are battered by the waves of trouble, we can expect God to understand and to comfort us in our distress. His Word, like a buoyant life preserver, holds us up in the bad times. But the life preserver only works if you put it on *before* your boat sinks. God will surround you with His love and protection—even if you're unconscious of His presence. He promises to keep our heads above water in the storms of living.

Preserving God, I cling to You as my life preserver. Keep my head above the turbulent waters so I don't drown. Bring me safely to the shore. Amen.

LOOKING FORWARD

*I focus on this one thing:
Forgetting the past and looking
forward to what lies ahead.*

PHILIPPIANS 3:13 NLT

As followers of Christ, we are people who look forward rather than backward. We have all made mistakes, but God does not want us to dwell on them, wallowing in guilt and discouragement. Instead, He calls us to let go of the past, trusting Him to deal with it. His grace is new every moment.

Father, I sometimes ruminate over past mistakes. Help me not to wallow in the past—instead, enable me to delight in Your grace, which is new each moment. Amen.

At All Times

*Pray in the Spirit at all times
and on every occasion.*
Ephesians 6:18 NLT

God wants to be included in our days. He wants to walk and talk with us each moment. Imagine if we traveled through the day with our children or our spouse, but we only spoke to them between 6:15 and 6:45 a.m! Of course we'd never do that to the people we care about. God doesn't want us to do that to Him either.

God wants to travel the journey

with us. He's a wonderful companion, offering wisdom and comfort for every aspect of our lives. But He can only do that if we let Him into our schedules, every minute of every day.

Dear Father, thank You for always being there to listen. Remind me to talk to You about everything, all the time. Amen.

POWER-PACKED
AND PERSONAL

••

Thou hast magnified thy
word above all thy name.
PSALM 138:2 KJV

••

Of all the wonderful graces and gifts
God has given humankind, there's
nothing that touches the power and
truth of that all-time bestseller, the
Bible. The Bible provides healing,
hope, and direction (Psalm 107:20;
119:74, 133). If we want wisdom
and the desire to do things the right
way, God's Word equips us for that

(2 Timothy 3:16–17). From the scriptures we can make sense of a confusing world. We can get a hold on real truth. God has given us His eternal Word to know Him and to know ourselves better.

Teach me not only to read, but also to obey Your living, powerful Word every day, Lord God. Amen.

A Shadow of the Past

"Only Rahab the prostitute and all who are with her in her house shall be spared, because she hid the spies we sent."
JOSHUA 6:17 NIV

Rahab wasn't trapped by her past. It didn't hold her back. She was used by God. Her name has come down to us centuries later because of her bold faith. We all have to deal with a past. But God is able to bring good from a painful past. By the grace and power of God we can make choices in the present that can affect our future. There is transforming power with God. We have hope, no matter what lies behind us.

Holy Spirit, You are always at work. Don't ever stop! Show me a new way, Lord. Help me to make healthier choices for myself and my family. Thank You for Your renewing presence in my life. Amen.

Peace Rules

Let the peace that comes from Christ rule in your hearts. For as members of one body you are called to live in peace.
Colossians 3:15 NLT

Peace is a way of living our lives. It happens when we let Christ's peace into our lives to rule over our emotions, our doubts, and our worries, and then go one step more and let His peace control the way we live. Peace is God's gift of grace to us, but it is also the way to a graceful life, the path to harmony with the world around us.

Jesus, what an amazing gift of peace that comes from You. Thank You for leading me on the path of a graceful life. Amen.

Praying Together

For where two or three are gathered together in my name, there am I in the midst of them.

Matthew 18:20 KJV

Of all the passages in the Bible that emphasize the importance of gathering for worship and prayer, this one stands out. It is short and sweet and to the point. Why should we gather together to pray with other Christians? Because when we do, *God shows up!* The Lord is in our midst.

As you gather with other Christians

in your church or even in your family, God is honored. He loves to listen to the hearts and voices of His children unified in prayer. He will be faithful to answer according to His perfect will.

Father, thank You for the promise that where we gather in Your name, there You will be also. Help me never to give up the practice of praying with fellow believers. Amen.

STANDING STILL

"The LORD will fight for you;
you need only to be still."
EXODUS 14:14 NIV

Moses commanded the Israelites to stop panicking and stand still. Then God held back the waters of the Red Sea, and the Israelites were able to walk across on dry ground! When the Egyptians tried to follow them, the waters rushed in and drowned them all.

Sometimes when we stress and panic, we rack our brains trying to figure out solutions to our problems;

and instead of standing still and praying to God, we become even more panicked. Moses' words still apply to us today. When we face our fears we should be still, trusting in God and relying on Him to bring us through the struggle.

Dear Lord, please teach me to be still and to trust in You. Thank You for Your constant faithfulness. Amen.

PERFECTION

I don't mean to say that I have already achieved these things or that I have already reached perfection. But I press on to possess that perfection for which Christ Jesus first possessed me.

PHILIPPIANS 3:12 NLT

We are called to be perfect. Nothing else is good enough for God's people. That doesn't mean we have an inflated sense of our own worth. And it doesn't mean we beat ourselves up when we fall short of perfection. We know that in our own strength we can never hope to achieve perfection—but with God's grace, anything is possible.

Jesus, when I am weary, give me the strength to keep pressing forward toward perfection. I want, more than anything, to be like You. Fill me with Your grace. Amen.

....

God left nothing that is not subject to them. Yet at present we do not see everything subject to them. But we do see Jesus.

HEBREWS 2:8–9 NIV

....

We know that Jesus has won the victory over sin, and yet when we look at the world as it is right now, we still see sin all around us. We see pain and suffering, greed and selfishness, brokenness and despair. We know that the world is not ruled by God. Yet despite that, we can look past the darkness of sin. By grace, right now, we can see Jesus.

Jesus, when I am overwhelmed by the evil that seems to be winning in this world, remind me that You have won the victory. Give me the grace to see You. Amen.

POWERFUL PRAYING

Therefore confess your sins to each other and pray for each other so that you may be healed. The prayer of a righteous person is powerful and effective.
JAMES 5:16 NIV

When we have God's approval, when we live with integrity and faith, He listens to us. But when we consistently make poor choices and disregard God's guidance, He may not take our prayers as seriously.

Oh, He will never take His love from

us, no matter what. And He will always listen when we ask for help out of our sin. But if we want our prayers to hold extra power, we need to live righteously. When we have God's approval on our lives, we can also know we have God's ear about all sorts of things. When we walk in God's will, we have access to God's power.

Dear Father, I want my prayers to be powerful and effective. Help me to live in a way that pleases You. Amen.

Rock Solid

"Therefore everyone who hears these words of mine and puts them into practice is like a wise man who built his house on the rock. The rain came down, the streams rose, and the winds blew and beat against that house; yet it did not fall, because it had its foundation on the rock."
MATTHEW 7:24–25 NIV

Prepare for tomorrow's storms by laying a solid foundation today. Rain and wind are guaranteed to come. It is only a matter of time. We need to be ready. When our foundation is the Rock, Jesus Christ, we will find ourselves still standing when the storm has passed.

Rain will come. Winds will blow and beat hard against us. Yet, when our hope is in the Lord, we will not be destroyed. We will remain steadfast because our feet have been firmly planted. Stand upon the Rock today so that your tomorrows will be secure.

*Dear Lord, help me build my
foundation today upon You
so I can remain steadfast in
the storms of life. Amen.*

Board God's Boat

Then, because so many people were coming and going that they did not even have a chance to eat, he said to them, "Come with me by yourselves to a quiet place and get some rest."

Mark 6:31 NIV

The apostles ministered tirelessly—so much so, they had little time to eat. The Lord noticed that they had neglected to take time for themselves. Sensitive to their needs, the Savior instructed them to retreat by boat with

Him to a solitary place of rest where He was able to minister to them. Often we allow the hectic pace of daily life to drain us physically and spiritually, and in the process, we deny ourselves time alone to pray and read God's Word. Meanwhile, God patiently waits. So perhaps it's time to board God's boat to a quieter place!

Heavenly Father, in my hectic life I've neglected time apart with You. Help me to board Your boat and stay afloat through spending time in Your Word and in prayer. Amen.

MOVE ON

Anyone who belongs to Christ has become a new person. The old life is gone; a new life has begun!
2 CORINTHIANS 5:17 NLT

You are a brand-new person in Jesus! Don't worry about what came before. Don't linger over your guilt and regret. Move on. Step out into the new, grace-filled life Christ has given you.

Heavenly Father, how grateful I am for new life! Thank You for putting to death the old me and for giving me the promise of a new life in Christ. Amen.

Bringing Us to Completion

"Being confident of this, that he who began a good work in you will carry it on to completion until the day of Christ Jesus."

Philippians 1:6 NIV

No matter how many times we fail, no matter how many times we mess up, we know God hasn't written us off. He's still working on us. He still loves us. Those of us who have been adopted into God's family through believing in His Son, Jesus Christ, can be confident that God won't give up on us. No matter how messed up our lives may seem, He will continue working in us until His plan is fulfilled, and we stand before Him, perfect and complete.

Dear Father, thank You for not giving up on me. Help me to cooperate with Your process of fulfilling Your purpose in me. Amen.

God's Work

The Lord will perfect that which concerns me; Your mercy, O Lord, endures forever; do not forsake the works of Your hands.
Psalm 138:8 NKJV

The psalmist offers hope when he tells us the Lord will complete things that concern us. We are the work of His hands and He has enduring mercy toward our failures. He is as active in our sanctification as He is in our salvation. Philippians 1:6 (NKJV) says, "Being confident of this very thing, that

He who has begun a good work in you will complete it until the day of Jesus Christ." The power to change or to see difficult things through to the end comes from the Lord who promises to complete the work He begins.

Lord, remind me of this word when I am discouraged by my lack of progress. Help me remember Your eternal love and mercy to me. Give me confidence that You will complete me. Amen.

A Child in Need

•••

"For all those things My hand has made, and all those things exist,"
says the LORD. "But on this one will I look: on him who is poor and of a contrite spirit, and who trembles at My word."
ISAIAH 66:2 NKJV

•••

A humble child of God with a need catches His eye. Though He is always watching over all of us, He is drawn to a child who needs Him. We may need forgiveness, wisdom, courage, endurance, patience, health, protection, or even love. God promises to come to our aid when He sees us with a hand up, reaching for His assistance. What needs do you have in your life today? Raise your hand in prayer to God. He'll take care of your needs, and then some—blessing your life in ways you can't even imagine!

Father, thank You for caring about the needs of Your children. Help me to remember to always seek You first. Amen.

QUIET, GENTLE GRACE

"Let me teach you, because I am humble and gentle at heart, and you will find rest for your souls."

MATTHEW 11:29 NLT

Sometimes we keep trying to do things on our own, even though we don't know what we're doing and even though we're exhausted. And all the while, Jesus waits quietly, ready to show us the way. He will lead us with quiet, gentle grace, carrying our burdens for us. We don't have to try so hard. We can finally rest.

Jesus, I don't like feeling incompetent and inadequate. It makes me feel anxious and exhausted. Thank You for Your gentle teaching and for the strength You provide. Give me Your rest. Amen.

What If?

The Lord will keep you from all harm—he will watch over your life.
PSALM 121:7 NIV

Feeling safe and secure rests not in the world or in other human beings but with God alone. He is a Christian's help and hope in every frightening situation. He promises to provide peace to everyone who puts their faith and trust in Him. What are you afraid of today? Allow God to encourage you. Trust Him to bring you through it and to give you peace.

Dear Lord, hear my prayers,
soothe me with Your Words,
and give me peace. Amen.

*"In this world you will have
trouble. But take heart!
I have overcome the world."*
John 16:33 NIV

Christ tells us to hold on to the hope
we have in Him. He tells us to "take
heart" because the trials of this world
have already been won, the evil has
already been conquered, and He has
already overcome the world. Live
your life as a statement of hope, not
despair. Live like the victor, not the
victim. Live with your eye on eternity,

not the here and now. Daily remind yourself that you serve a powerful and gracious God, and decide to be used by Him to act as a messenger of grace and healing to the world's brokenness.

Lord, forgive my doubts. Forgive me for growing discouraged and not placing my full trust in You. May I learn to trust You better and to live my life as a statement of hope. Amen.

THE SECRET OF SERENDIPITY

....

*A happy heart makes
the face cheerful.*
PROVERBS 15:13 NIV

....

Can you remember the last time you laughed in wild abandon? Better yet, when was the last time you did something fun, outrageous, or out of the ordinary? Perhaps it is an activity you haven't done since you were a child, like slip down a waterslide, strap on a pair of ice skates, or pitch a tent and camp overnight. A happy heart turns life's situations into opportunities for fun. When we seek innocent pleasures, we glean the benefits of a happy heart. So try a bit of whimsy just for fun. And rediscover the secret of serendipity.

Dear Lord, because of You, I have a happy heart. Lead me to do something fun and spontaneous today! Amen.

What's Real

*"Then you will experience
for yourselves the truth,
and the truth will free you."*
John 8:32 MSG

Truth is what is real, while lies are nothing but words. God wants us to experience what is truly real. Sometimes we would rather hide from reality, but grace comes to us through truth. No matter how painful the truth may seem sometimes, it will ultimately set us free.

Jesus, thank You for the truth that sets me free. Help me to discern truth from lies. Allow me to experience Your truth in the depth of my being. Amen.

SHOUTS OF JOY

. . . .

"He will yet fill your mouth
with laughter and your
lips with shouts of joy."
JOB 8:21 NIV

. . . .

Do you remember the last time you laughed till you cried? For many of us, it's been far too long. Stress tends to steal our joy, leaving us humorless and oh-so-serious. But lightness and fun haven't disappeared forever. They may be buried beneath the snow of a long, wintery life season, but spring is coming. Laughter will bloom again,

and our hearts will soar as our lips
shout with joy. Grasp that hope!

Father God, thank You for the
hope of joy. I know that because
I trust in You, as sure as spring
follows winter, joy will again
bloom in my heart. Amen.

Rescued

God rescued us from dead-end alleys and dark dungeons. He's set us up in the kingdom of the Son he loves so much, the Son who got us out of the pit we were in, got rid of the sins we were doomed to keep repeating.
COLOSSIANS 1:13–14 MSG

The message of the Gospel doesn't leave us trapped in our sin and misery without hope. God sent the rescuer, Christ, who plucked us out of the dungeons of despair and into His kingdom of light and strength to overcome the dragons of sin. It's by the Father's grace that we are not stuck in our habitual ruts and dead-end alleys, living without purpose and fulfillment. We walk in His kingdom—a kingdom that goes counter to the world's ideas. We are out of the pit, striding confidently in Him, enjoying life to its fullest.

Glory to You, Jesus! You have rescued me from the pit and lifted me to Your kingdom of real life and victory. Help me to walk in that fact today. Amen.

A Very Important Phrase

....

And it came to pass. . .
Found More Than 400 Times
in the King James Bible

....

There are times in life when we think we can't bear one more day, one more hour, one more minute. But no matter how bad things seem at the time, they are temporary. What's really important is how we handle the opportunities before us today, whether we let our trials defeat us or look for the hand of God in everything. Every day, week, and year are made up of things that "come to pass"—so even if we fail, we needn't be disheartened. Other opportunities—better days— will come. Let's look past those hard things today and glorify the name of the Lord.

Lord Jesus, how awesome it is that You send or allow these little things that will pass. May we recognize Your hand in them today and praise You for them. Amen.

Grace Multiplied

*Honor the LORD with your
wealth and with the best part
of everything you produce.*
PROVERBS 3:9 NLT

We connect the word *wealth* with money, but long ago the word meant "happiness, prosperity, well-being." If you think about your wealth in this light, then the word encompasses far more of your life. Your health, your abilities, your friends, your family, your physical strength, and your creative energy—all of these are parts of your true wealth. Grace brought all of these riches into your life, and when we use them to honor God, grace is multiplied still more.

Father, when I consider all the good things You have given me, I am rich beyond belief. Help me to graciously honor You with my wealth. Amen.

Everyday Blessings

But the eyes of the Lord are on those who fear him, on those whose hope is in his unfailing love.
Psalm 33:18 NIV

The Lord of all creation is watching our every moment and wants to fill us with His joy. He often interrupts our lives with His blessings: butterflies dancing in sunbeams, dew-touched spiderwebs, cotton candy clouds, and glorious crimson sunsets. The beauty of His creation reassures us of His unfailing love and fills us with hope.

But it is up to us to take the time to notice.

Dear heavenly Father, the next time I spot butterflies dancing in sunbeams, please remind me to whisper a quick thank-You for Your amazing creation. Amen.

Joyful, Patient, and Faithful

••

*Be joyful in hope, patient in
affliction, faithful in prayer.*
Romans 12:12 NIV

••

Faithfulness in prayer requires
discipline. God is faithful regardless
of our attitude toward Him. He never
changes, wavers, or forsakes His
own. We may be faithful to do daily
tasks around the house. We feed the
cat, wash the clothes, and empty the
trash. But faithfulness in the quiet
discipline of prayer is harder. There

are seemingly no consequences for neglecting our time with the Lord. Oh, what a myth this is! Set aside a daily time for prayer, and see how the Lord blesses you, transforming your spirit to increase your joyful hope, your patience, and your faithfulness.

Faithful God, find me faithful.
Stir up the hope and joy within
me. Give me the grace I need
to wait on You. Amen.

THE WHITE KNIGHT

....

*Then I will rejoice in the LORD. I will
be glad because he rescues me.*

PSALM 35:9 NLT

....

We're all waiting for someone to
rescue us. We wait and wait and wait
. . . The truth is, God doesn't want you
to exist in a perpetual state of waiting.
Live your life—your whole life—by
seeking daily joy in the Savior of your
soul, Jesus Christ. And here's the
best news of all: He's already done
the rescuing by dying on the cross for
our sins! He's the *true* white knight

who secured your eternity in heaven.
Stop waiting; seek His face today!

*Jesus, I praise You because
You are the rescuer of my soul.
Remind me of this fact when I'm
looking for relief in other people
and places. You take care of my
present and eternal needs, and
for that I am grateful. Amen.*

Heaven's Perspective

*Always give yourselves
fully to the work of the Lord,
because you know that your
labor in the Lord is not in vain.*
1 Corinthians 15:58 NIV

You may feel sometimes as though all
of your hard work comes to nothing.
But if your work is the Lord's work, you
can trust Him to bring it to fulfillment.
You may not always know what is being
accomplished in the light of eternity,
but God knows. And when you look
back from heaven's perspective, you

will be able to see how much grace
was accomplished through all of your
hard work.

*God, when I don't see results,
I sometimes get discouraged in
my work for You. Help me to
remember that You are busy doing
things I cannot see. Amen.*

A Little Goes a Long Way

"The Lord our God has allowed a few of us to survive as a remnant."
Ezra 9:8 NLT

Remnants. Useless by most standards, but God is in the business of using tiny slivers of what's left to do mighty things. Nehemiah rebuilt the fallen walls of Jerusalem with a remnant of Israel; Noah's three sons repopulated the earth after the flood; four slave boys—Daniel, Shadrach, Meshach, and Abednego—kept faith alive for an entire nation. When it feels as if bits and pieces are all that has survived of your hope, remember how much God can accomplish with remnants!

Father God, thank You for proving that there is hope. . . even in the remnants! Amen.

Unbroken Promise

*In hope of eternal life
which God, who cannot lie,
promised before time began.*
Titus 1:2 NKJV

God always keeps His word. The Bible is filled with the promises of God—vows to us that we can trust will be completed. God never lies. Lying is not in Him. He sees us as worthy of His commitment. The promise of eternal life—given even before time began—is one of God's most wonderful gifts. No matter how disappointed we are with ourselves or with others, we only have to look at the pledge God has made to be filled with a heart of praise and gladness.

God, thank You that Your Word is trustworthy and true. Praise You for the promise of eternal life. Amen.

NOTHING MORE VALUABLE

∙∙

"Wisdom is more valuable than gold and crystal. It cannot be purchased with jewels mounted in fine gold."
JOB 28:17 NLT

∙∙

Money can't buy you love—and it can't buy wisdom either. Wisdom is more precious than anything this world has to offer. In fact, some passages of the Old Testament seem to indicate that Wisdom is another name for Jesus. Just as Jesus is the Way, the Truth, and the Life, He is also the One who gives us the vision to see God's world all around us. No other gift is more valuable than Jesus.

Jesus, the Way, the Truth, and the Life, give me Your vision. Help me to see the world through Your eyes. Help me to place my relationship with You above all else. Amen.

A Solid Foundation

*A bad motive can't
achieve a good end.*
PROVERBS 17:20 MSG

We hear it all the time: The end justifies the means. But that is not how it works in the kingdom of God. It's like trying to build a beautiful house on a shaky foundation. It just doesn't work. Sooner or later, the weak foundation will affect the rest of the house. True achievement is built on God's grace and love. That is the kind of foundation that holds solid no matter what.

Father, fill my heart with the longing and motivation to do Your work. Help me to build that work on the solid foundation of Your grace and love. Amen.

Increasing Visibility

"Where then is my hope?"
Job 17:15 NIV

. . . .

On hectic days when fatigue takes its toll, when we feel like cornless husks, hope disappears. When hurting people hurt people, and we're in the line of fire, hope vanishes. When ideas fizzle, efforts fail; when we throw the spaghetti against the wall and nothing sticks, hope seems lost. But we must remember it's only temporary. The mountaintop isn't gone just because it's obscured by fog. Visibility will improve tomorrow and hope will rise.

God of Hope, I am thankful to know You. . .and to trust that because of You, hope will rise. Amen.

A Matter of Priorities

To everything there is a season, a time for every purpose under heaven.
Ecclesiastes 3:1 NKJV

Only one thing in our lives never changes: God. When our world swirls and threatens to shift out of control, we can know that God is never surprised, never caught off guard by anything that happens. Just as He guided David through dark nights and Joseph through his time in prison, God can show us a secure way through any difficulty. He can turn the roughest times to good. Just as He supported His servants in times past, He will always be with us, watching and loving.

Lord, help me remember Your love and guidance when my life turns upside down. Grant me wisdom for the journey and a hope for the future. Amen.

A Comfortable Place

Don't you realize that your body is the temple of the Holy Spirit, who lives in you and was given to you by God? You do not belong to yourself.
1 CORINTHIANS 6:19 NLT

We take the time to make our homes comfortable and beautiful when we know visitors are coming. In the same way, we ought to prepare our hearts for the Holy Spirit who lives inside of us. We should daily ask God to help us clean up the junk in our hearts. We should take special care to tune up our bodies through exercise, eating healthful foods, and dressing attractively and modestly. Our bodies belong to God. Taking care of ourselves shows others that we honor God enough to respect and use wisely what He has given us.

Dear Lord, thank You for letting me belong to You. May my body be a comfortable place for You. Amen.

FOCUS POINT

....

Therefore. . .stand firm.
Let nothing move you.
1 CORINTHIANS 15:58 NIV

....

Some days stress comes at us from all directions. Our emotions are overwhelming. Life makes us dizzy. On days like that, don't worry about getting a lot accomplished—and don't try to make enormous leaps in your spiritual life. Instead, simply stand in one place. Like a ballet dancer who looks at one point to keep her balance while she twirls, fix your eyes on Jesus.

Jesus, when I get caught up in the whirlwind of stress and busyness and my own agenda, I can easily lose my balance. Help me to fix my eyes on You. Amen.

SMILING IN THE DARKNESS

*"The hopes of the
godless evaporate."*
JOB 8:13 NLT

Hope isn't just an emotion; it's a perspective, a discipline, a way of life. It's a journey of choice. We must learn to override those messages of discouragement, despair, and fear that assault us in times of trouble and press toward the light. Hope is smiling in the darkness. It's confidence that faith in God's

sovereignty amounts to something. . .
something life-changing, life-saving,
and eternal.

Father God, help me smile
through the darkness today.
Thank You for hope. Amen.

Remember This

....

Keep your eyes on Jesus,
who both began and
finished this race we're in.
HEBREWS 12:2 MSG

....

When our heads are spinning and tears are flowing, there is only one thing to remember: focus on Jesus. He will never leave you nor forsake you. When you focus on Him, His presence envelops you. Where there is despair, He imparts hope. Where there is fear, He imparts faith. Where there is worry, He imparts peace. He will lead you on the right path and grant you wisdom for the journey. When the unexpected trials of life come upon you, remember this: focus on Jesus.

Dear Lord, I thank You that nothing takes You by surprise. When I am engulfed in the uncertainties of life, help me remember to focus on You. Amen.

ONE THING IS NEEDED

"Martha, Martha," the Lord answered, "you are worried and upset about many things, but few things are needed—or indeed only one."
LUKE 10:41–42 NIV

We are each given twenty-four hours in a day. Einstein and Edison were given no more than Joseph and Jeremiah of the Old Testament. Since God has blessed each of us with twenty-four hours, let's seek His direction on how to spend this invaluable commodity wisely—giving more attention to people than things, spending more time on relationships than the rat race. In Luke, our Lord reminded dear, dogged, drained Martha that only one thing is needed—Him.

Father God, oftentimes I get caught up in the minutia of life. The piled laundry can appear more important than the people around me. Help me to use my time wisely. Open my eyes to see what is truly important. Amen.

For the word of God is alive and powerful. It is sharper than the sharpest two-edged sword, cutting between soul and spirit, between joint and marrow. It exposes our innermost thoughts and desires.

Hebrews 4:12 NLT

God's words are not merely letters on a page. They are living things that work their way into our hearts and minds, revealing the fears and hopes we've kept hidden away, sometimes even from ourselves. Like a doctor's scalpel that cuts in order to heal, God's Word slices through our carefully created facades and exposes our deepest truths.

Father, how grateful I am for Your Word. I am amazed at the way it teaches me and exposes my true intentions. Help me to bravely submit myself to Your healing. Amen.

Small but Mighty

"He has. . .exalted the humble."
LUKE 1:52 NLT

God delights in making small things great. He's in the business of taking scrap-heap people and turning them into treasures: Noah (the laughing-stock of his city), Moses (stuttering shepherd turned national leader), David (smallest among the big and powerful), Sarah (old and childless), Mary (poor teenager), Rahab (harlot turned faith-filled ancestor of Jesus). So you and I can rejoice with hope! Let us glory in our smallness!

I feel so very small today, God. Please remind me that because I am Yours, I am worthy. And that's all that matters! Amen.

UNSWERVING FAITH

Let us hold unswervingly to the hope we profess, for he who promised is faithful.

HEBREWS 10:23 NIV

The author of Hebrews challenges us to hold *unswervingly* to our hope in Christ Jesus. Certainly we fail to do this at times, but life is much better when we keep our eyes fixed on Him. Sometimes just a whisper from Satan, the father of lies, can cause shakiness where once there was steadfastness. Place your hope in Christ alone. He will help you to resist the lies of this world. Hold *unswervingly* to your Savior today. He is faithful!

Jesus, You are the object of my hope. There are many distractions in my life, but I pray that You will help me to keep my eyes on You. Thank You for Your faithfulness. Amen.

Who Helps the Helper?

*The Lord is my strength and my
shield; my heart trusted in him, and
I am helped: therefore my heart
greatly rejoiceth; and with my
song will I praise him.*
Psalm 28:7 kjv

Helping can be exhausting. The
needs of young children, teens,
grandchildren, aging parents,
our neighbors, and fellow church
members—the list is never ending—
can stretch us until we're ready to
snap. And then we find that *we* need

help. Who helps the helper? The Lord does. When we are weak, He is strong. When we are vulnerable, He is our shield. When we can no longer trust in our own resources, we can trust in Him. He is always there, ready to help. Rejoice in Him, praise His name, and you will find the strength to go on.

Father, I'm worn out. I can't care for all the people and needs You bring into my life by myself. I need Your strength. Thank You for being my helper and my shield. Amen.

BLESSING OTHERS

"Bless those who curse you.
Pray for those who hurt you."
LUKE 6:28 NLT

Not only does God bless us, but we are called to bless others. God wants to show the world His grace through us. He can do this when we show our commitment to make God's love real in the world around us through our words and actions, as well as through our prayer life. We offer blessings to others when we greet a scowl with a smile, when we refuse to respond to angry words, and when we offer understanding to those who are angry and hurt.

God, I sometimes forget that the world is watching. I long to shine Your light to everyone I see. Help me to bestow blessings on others, even when they hurt me. Amen.

Go for It

When everything was hopeless, Abraham believed anyway, deciding to live. . .on what God said he would do.

Romans 4:18 msg

"You can't do that. It's impossible." Have you ever been told this? Or just thought it because of fear or a previous experience with failure? This world is full of those who discourage rather than encourage. If we believe them, we'll never do anything. But if we, like Abraham, believe that God has called us for a particular purpose, we'll go for it despite our track records. Past failure doesn't dictate future failure. If God wills it, He fulfills it.

Help me to have the faith of Abraham, Father God. . . to believe anyway! Amen.

Try 3-Minute Prayers!

3-Minute Prayers for Women

This devotional prayer title packs a powerful dose of inspiration into just-right-sized readings for women of all ages and stages. Each prayer, written specifically for devotional quiet time, meets readers right where they are—and is complemented by a relevant scripture and question for further thought.

Paperback / 978-1-68322-317-7 / $4.99